# Discovering

# FLIES

**Christopher O'Toole**

Illustrations by Wendy Meadway

The Bookwright Press
New York · 1987

# Discovering Nature

Discovering Ants
Discovering Bees and Wasps
Discovering Beetles
Discovering Birds of Prey
Discovering Butterflies and Moths
Discovering Crickets and Grasshoppers
Discovering Flies

Discovering Frogs and Toads
Discovering Rabbits and Hares
Discovering Snakes and Lizards
Discovering Spiders
Discovering Squirrels
Discovering Worms

**Further titles are in preparation**

All photographs from Oxford Scientific Films

First published in the
United States in 1987 by
The Bookwright Press
387 Park Avenue South
New York, NY 10016

First published in 1986 by
Wayland (Publishers) Limited
61 Western Road, Hove
East Sussex, BN3 1JD, England

© Copyright 1986 Wayland (Publishers) Limited

ISBN 0-531-18097-2
Library of Congress Catalog Card Number: 86-71272

Typeset by Alphabet Typesetters Limited
Printed in Italy by Sagdos S.p.A., Milan

Cover *A greenbottle is a very colorful fly. The females lay their eggs on animal remains and droppings.*

Frontispiece *The crane fly looks somewhat like a mosquito.*

# Contents

# 1
# What are Flies?

*A horsefly on a leaf. Only the females of this kind of fly bite.*

## Introducing Flies

Flies are a very important group of insects; there are about 150,000 different kinds in the world. **True flies** have only one pair of wings. We call them true flies because not all of the insects that have "fly" as part of their name are really flies. Butterflies, mayflies and sawflies are not true flies. These insects all have two pairs of wings.

Flies include such common insects as bluebottles, houseflies, flower flies, mosquitoes and midges. There are hundreds of different ways that flies can make a living. Some, like flower flies, eat the **pollen** and **nectar** of flowers and are useful as **pollinators**. Other flies catch a wide range of insects and eat them. They are useful to us because they kill a lot of pests. But flies can be pests themselves. In their grub stages, many kinds damage crops; mosquitoes and

tsetse flies are harmful to humans because they suck blood and can pass on bad diseases.

Whether or not they are nuisances, many flies are very beautiful. They are often brightly colored, with pretty patterns on their wings and bodies.

*The deer fly has a definite pattern on its wings and colorful eyes. Like the horsefly, female deer flies bite to suck blood.*

Some are very strange indeed, like those whose grubs live in pools of oil and others that live in hot springs.

*A close-up of the head of a horsefly showing its piercing mouthparts. Its large, colorful eyes are made up of hundreds of little facets.*

## The Fly's Body

Like all adult insects, flies have bodies made up of three parts – the head, the **thorax** and the **abdomen**.

The easiest things to see on a fly's head are the eyes. Each one is made up of hundreds, or even thousands, of little eyes called facets. The head also bears the **antennae**, or feelers, which are sensitive to touch and smell. Some flies have feathery antennae, which are also used as ears.

All flies have sucking mouthparts and feed on liquid food. The tongue is tube-shaped, and muscles in the head make it work like a pump.

The thorax bears six legs, and two wings and contains all the muscles that work them. At the tip of each foot is a pair of claws, each with a sticky pad that enables the fly to walk on smooth surfaces such as ceilings and window panes. The thorax also bears a pair of

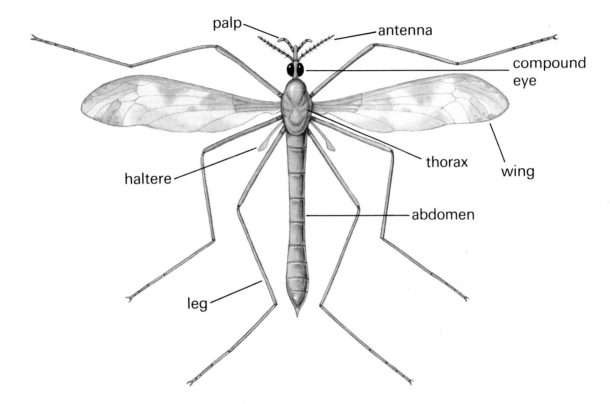

The body of a crane fly showing all its major parts labeled. Crane flies have long legs, slender wings and narrow bodies.

haltere just behind the wings. These are shaped like little drum sticks and are the remains of the hind pair of wings. The ancestors of flies once had two pairs of wings, but the hind pair has changed into the halteres, which help the fly to keep its balance.

The abdomen of a fly contains the stomach and the parts that make the female's eggs or the male's **sperm**.

# 2
# The Life History of Flies

*An adult housefly, its wings still crumpled, just after it has emerged from the pupa.*

## How Flies Grow

All flies pass through three stages before becoming adult: the egg, **larva**, and **pupa**. The larva, or grub stage, is the same as the caterpillar stage in butterflies and moths and the pupa is the same as the chrysalis stage.

A female housefly lays between 100 and 150 eggs per day, always on something suitable for her larvae to eat. Bad smelling, rotting material like dung, dead animals and garbage around people's homes, is ideal "food."

Each egg is white and about the size of a pinhead. It hatches in half to one and a half days, depending on the temperature, into a legless larva. The larva does not like light and soon burrows down into the food. It has a pair of hooks at its mouth end and a pair of breathing holes, or **spiracles**, at its rear end. The larva feeds greedily and grows quickly. The larval stage lasts between five and twenty-six days, and in this time the skin is shed three times.

At the last skin change, the larva becomes a pupa. It remains inside this skin, which hardens and becomes reddish brown. This skin is called a **puparium**. Only the most highly evolved flies have this. Flies like the crane fly have a naked pupa, and you can see its wings and legs as they grow. The pupal stage lasts between four and twenty-three days, after which the adult fly emerges. At first it has crumpled wings, but these are soon pumped up with blood, and the new housefly flies away.

*The life cycle of a housefly.*

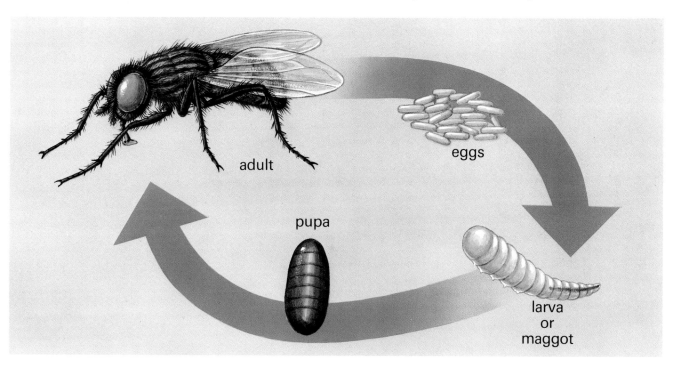

adult

eggs

pupa

larva
or
maggot

## Growing Up Under Water

Many of the wiggly, squiggly things you find in ponds are the larvae of flies. As larvae, they spend all their time under the water and emerge into the air only when they become adult.

You can find some, like the larva of the common gnat, in barrels of rain water. The female gnat lays about 200 eggs, which float on the water like a raft. Each larva hatches from the egg directly into

*Mosquito larvae breathe through a tube, which they stick into the air above the surface of the water.*

the water. It swims with a fast, jerky movement. The larva breathes through a tube, or **siphon**, which it sticks out into the air. The larva eats tiny, single-celled plants and animals. It sweeps them into its mouth with two brushes of hairs.

The gnat pupa is comma-shaped and does not form a puparium like the housefly. It too can swim with a jerky action. It breathes at the surface of the water through a pair of trumpet-shaped siphons on its thorax.

Just before the adult gnat is about to emerge, the pupa lies flat beneath the water's surface. Its thorax splits along the top and the adult gnat emerges into the air without getting wet. The new gnat stands on the surface of the water for a few minutes while its wings harden and then it flies off.

*An adult mosquito emerges from the pupa directly into the air.*

*A mosquito pupa swimming. It breathes at the surface of the water through two tubes.*

## Growing Up on Land

Many fly larvae grow and feed in the soil or on the surface of the ground. Some feed on small soil animals, others in the roots of plants. There is even one kind

*The larva of a crane fly is sometimes called a leatherjacket because of its leathery skin.*

of fly larvae that lives inside the bodies of earthworms, slowly eating their insides.

Some soil-living larvae are called leatherjackets because they have a gray, leathery skin. They are the larvae of crane flies, which have long legs and slender bodies. Leatherjackets are pests because they eat the roots of grass, wheat and even young trees. Some crane fly larvae live in rotten wood.

Not all fly larvae are pests. Many kinds of flower flies are useful to farmers and gardeners because they eat vast numbers of **aphids**. The young flower fly eats about three or four aphids a day. When it is older and larger, it can eat as many as one a minute. The larva is green and slug-like. It moves over leaves with a looping movement. When it finds an aphid, it impales it on its two mouth hooks. Then it rears up its front end and sucks the aphid dry.

*A flower fly larva eats an aphid by sucking out all its juices.*

# 3
# Flies, Plants and Animals

*Here you can see the larva and some eggs of the cabbage root fly.*

## Flies Harmful to Plants

The larvae of many kinds of flies eat plants. If you look on thistle flowers you may see some pretty, gray flies with dark patterns on their wings. The females have a very long **ovipositors**, or egg-laying tubes, at their rear ends. These are called thistle gall flies, and they lay their eggs in the stem of the thistle. The larvae burrow into the plant and cause a swelling, called a gall, on which they feed from the inside.

Other flies are a serious nuisance to farmers and gardeners because their larvae damage, and often kill, plant crops. The cabbage root fly is a good example. In spring, the females fly low over cabbage fields. They lay eggs on the cabbage stems near the soil or in cracks in the soil nearby. After hatching from the eggs, the larvae move to the cabbage roots. They feed inside slimy tunnels chewed in the root. There may be more

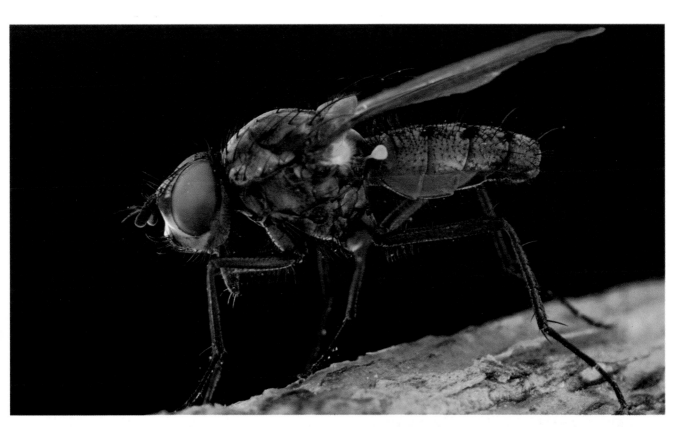

than one hundred larvae in a single
cabbage plant. The cabbage looks
sickly, wilts and usually dies.

After feeding, the larvae pupate
either in their tunnels or in the soil. The
new batch of flies appears in the
summer and the females fly off, after

*The cabbage root fly lays its eggs on or near
cabbage stems.*

**mating**, in search of more cabbage
plants. The cabbage root fly will attack
vegetables related to the cabbage, such
as radishes and turnips.

## Louse-flies

There are some very special flies called louse-flies. They live in the fur and feathers of animals and birds and suck their blood. Louse-flies have tough, flattened bodies and big claws for hanging on to their **hosts**.

Some louse-flies have wings, others do not. A few kinds shed their wings after they have found their host.

Louse-flies are choosy about their hosts; those that live on mammals, such as horses or sheep, never attack birds; and the kinds that live on birds never stray from their feathered hosts.

All louse-flies have one very peculiar thing in common. They do not lay eggs, nor do they have free-living larvae.

*This parasitic fly, found on a pigeon, has large claws to cling to its host.*

Instead, each female keeps one larva at a time inside her body. The larva eats a special liquid made by its mother. When the larva is fully grown, the mother lays it, sticking it to the fur or feathers of its host with a special kind of glue. The larva pupates immediately, and the puparium is round and looks like a small, brown pea.

*These five-day-old swifts have been attacked by blood-sucking louse-flies.*

One special louse-fly is found only on swifts. When the swifts are about to fly away to spend the winter in Africa, the female louse-fly lays her larva in the nest. The pupa waits there until the swifts return the following summer.

## Flies Harmful to Animals

Horseflies are a special group of fast-moving, blood-sucking flies. Some are very large and can grow to 25 mm (1 in) long, with a wingspan of 50 mm (2 in). Horseflies have very strong mouthparts for piercing the tough skins of horses and cattle. Only the females do this; the males drink nectar from flowers.

Warble flies cause much more serious harm to cattle. The females lay clumps of eggs on the underside of a cow. The larvae burrow through the skin and feed for two months inside the cow. Then they travel through the cow's body to the skin of its back. Here, they bite a breathing hole and stay for up to two months. These wounds cause the cow a lot of pain and they usually become infected. When the larvae are fully grown, they drop to the ground and pupate. In some hot countries, there are flies whose larvae live under the skin of humans.

*The sore on this cow's back is the breathing hole of a warble fly larva.*

The larvae of the horse botfly feed on the stomach linings of horses, mules and donkeys. They hatch from eggs laid on the horse's front legs and get into its mouth by hanging on to its lips when it grooms itself. Once inside the stomach, the larvae attach themselves to the

*Botflies on a horse's face. Their larvae feed inside the stomach linings of horses.*

stomach lining with their mouth hooks for nine to ten months. When they are ready to pupate, they let go and pass out with the horse's dung.

## Garbage-Loving Flies

There are many kinds of flies that eat dung and garbage. If you look at any fresh animal dropping you will see it covered with flies. The same is true of rotting meat and fish. The flies are attracted by the smell because it tells them that here is a place to eat and to lay eggs. Flies, especially houseflies and

*This housefly is feeding on the sugar on a doughnut. It has softened the sugar with saliva, to make it easy to eat.*

bluebottles, love to eat bad smelling, rotten things. Their mouthparts and feet become covered with lots of different kinds of germs.

Flies also like sweet things. After visiting all the rotting food, they may

come into our homes in search of sugar and cake. Here, they trample over food meant for us and leave invisible but germ-covered footprints.

When flies eat sweet things, like sugar, they soften it by spewing up some of their saliva. This is a sure way to spread any germs that are on their tongues. If we then eat the food, the germs carried by the flies can make us

*Three houseflies on a piece of tomato from a sandwich. You can see their spongelike mouthparts mopping up the food.*

very ill. They especially cause bad stomach upsets.

Germs could not find a better means of transportation than the housefly. For this reason, we should keep all our food covered.

## Malaria and Sleeping Sickness

Several kinds of flies cause disease in a very different way from that of the housefly and other, garbage-loving flies. These other flies spread diseases such as yellow fever, malaria and sleeping sickness when they suck our blood. And the disease germs are very special, too. They must spend part of their lives in a fly and the other part in the blood and liver of animals such as humans.

Malaria is one of these diseases, and

*The malaria cycle: 1. infected mosquito bites human; 2. parasite grows in human liver cells; 3. parasite enters red blood cells; 4. another mosquito bites human; 5. parasite grows in mosquito's stomach cells; 6. parasite enters mosquito's saliva.*

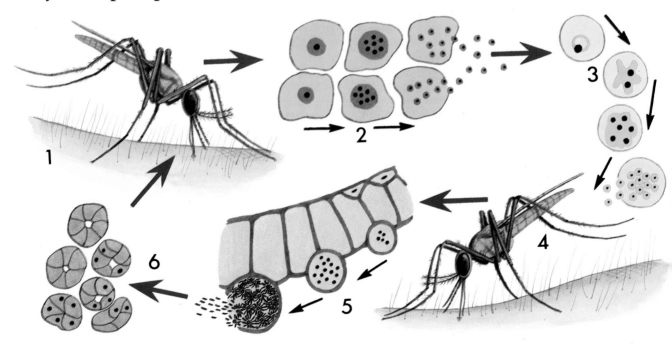

it is passed on by infected mosquitoes feeding on humans. Birds and other animals, especially apes, have their own kinds of malaria, all passed on by mosquitoes. A person with malaria feels very ill and has a very high temperature. This disease kills millions of people in hot countries each year. It used to be common in Europe, but has been wiped out by the draining of marshes in which the larvae of malaria-carrying mosquitoes live.

Another kind of disease, called sleeping sickness, is passed on by tsetse flies in Africa. It affects humans and also grazing animals such as cattle and antelopes. The tsetse fly looks like a housefly, but has a long, piercing tongue sticking out from the front of the head. Tsetse flies are like louse-flies in that the female lays a fully grown larva, which pupates immediately.

*A tsetse fly sucking blood from a person.*

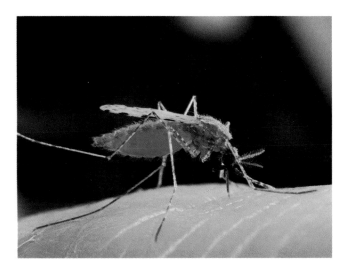

Above *A female mosquito sucking blood from a person's finger. Its abdomen is swollen with blood.*

# 4
# Useful Flies

*A yellow dungfly standing on dung. Female dungflies lay their eggs in manure, and their larvae eat it.*

## Dungflies and Scavengers

Not all flies are pests. Many are important members of the community of useful insects that live in dung. The common yellow dungfly is the easiest to see; every fresh cowpat has several sitting on it. Females lay eggs in the dung and the larvae feed on it.

But cowpats have other uses for dungflies. They are a meeting place for males and females: many of the dungflies you see will be mating. Adult dungflies eat a host of other flies that visit cowpats. They pounce on the flies and suck them dry.

Dungflies are useful because their larvae help to break down the dung and return nutrients to the soil. Flies that are **scavengers** on dead bodies are useful in the same way. Bluebottles and greenbottles, sometimes called blowflies, are very important because they get rid of corpses. A female finds a

dead body, say a mouse, very soon after death. She lays eggs on it and the larvae quickly burrow through the nostrils or eyesockets, into the mouse. Each one oozes digestive juices from its mouth, which break down the mouse's flesh and make it semi-liquid. The fly larvae

*A flesh fly deposits her larva in the mouth of a dead wood mouse. A greenbottle also shows interest in the corpse.*

then suck this up, feeding rapidly and together. Soon the body is reduced to a skeleton and a little bit of fur.

## Flies and Flowers

Bees are the main pollinators of flowering plants; however, flies are also important pollinators. Many have hairy bodies and are just as useful as bees for

*A flower fly feeding on nectar at a flower. Its striped abdomen makes it look like a wasp.*

carrying pollen from one plant to another. Flies have short tongues as a rule and find it easy to get at the nectar in small, open flower heads. Flower flies eat the pollen, and also drink the nectar of flowers.

Many flowers are specialized to attract flies and have a bad smell, like dung or rotting meat. This attracts those kinds of flies that lay their eggs in such things. A very strange plant that depends entirely on flies to pollinate it is the wild arum. This plant grows among shrubs and bushes and smells like something rotten. It also gives off heat, which makes the smell of decay waft out more quickly. Small flies are attracted to the flower and crawl inside. Once inside the plant they cannot escape because of a ring of hairs. While they are trapped, the male flowers, near the bottom, mature and dust the flies with pollen. The next day, the guard hairs wither and the flies escape. If they visit another arum plant, the pollen they are carrying will pollinate the female flowers of the arum.

*Several flower flies eating nectar and pollen on a flower. There are also several beetles on this flower.*

# 5
# Flies and Other Insects

*A robber fly eating a wasp. Robber flies have large eyes and long legs.*

## Hunting Flies

There are several groups of flies that are fierce hunters of other insects. The largest and commonest are called robber flies or assassin flies. They have big eyes and can fly very fast. You can often see them patrolling up and down the same beat, say, along a patch in a sandy area such as a dune. When a robber fly sees a suitable insect, it pounces on it and sinks its tough, piercing mouthparts into a soft part of the victim's body and sucks it dry.

Everything about the robber fly is geared to catching insects. It has very good eyesight and a piercing tongue. The legs hang down and forward and are covered with stiff bristles. This makes it easier for the robber fly to grab and hold onto flying insects. There are hundreds of different kinds of robber flies and most are found in the warmer parts of the world.

Some flies attack insects not only for food, but also to attract a mate. Male danceflies do this. They catch an insect, usually another fly, and may feed on it. But they do not suck it completely dry.

*An Australian robber fly eating another fly.*

Instead, they offer it to a female as a gift. While she feeds on it, the male mates with her.

## Bristly Parasites

Many flies grow as parasites of other insects. A parasite is an animal that lives at the expense of another animal, feeding slowly on it, but not usually killing it. Insect parasites usually do kill their hosts, and because of this, they are given a special name; we call them **parasitoids**. There is one group of bristly flies in which all the different kinds have larvae which are parasitoids of other insects. Only one fly larva develops in each host. Many kinds attack the caterpillars of moths and butterflies. Some attack beetles and a few even go for woodlice and centipedes.

There are several ways that the larvae of bristly parasites get into their victims. The females of some kinds lay eggs in or on the host. They may have a special ovipositor to do this. Others simply lay their eggs on leaves or on

*A parasitic fly on a field cricket. Its larva will feed and pupate inside the cricket.*

the surface of the soil. They rely on the host accidentally eating the egg. Once inside the insect, the egg hatches and the larva begins to eat the insides of the host. The females of some bristly parasites are like those of the louse-flies and tsetse flies because they lay

larvae instead of eggs. When a bristly parasite larva has finished feeding, it pupates inside the host's body.

*Inside this bee's abdomen there is a fly pupa. Before pupating the fly larva has eaten the bee's insides.*

*A bee fly scattering eggs around the nest burrows of mining bees. When the eggs hatch the larvae will feed on the mining bees' food.*

## Bee Flies and Satellite Flies

If you live in a cool climate you can sometimes find some very furry flies hovering over patches of bare earth in the spring. These are female bee flies, which are very bee-like in appearance. They have long tongues and a rapid, darting flight, and many kinds have dark patterns on their wings. If you see a female hovering, she is doing something very special. She is scattering lots of very tiny eggs around the nest burrows of mining bees.

The eggs hatch very quickly and the larvae move into the bee holes. There, they live as parasites, feeding on the bee larvae from the outside. Sometimes they also feed on the pollen stored by the mother bee.

When the larva of a bee fly has finished feeding, it travels to the soil surface and pupates just beneath it. The new bee fly appears the next spring.

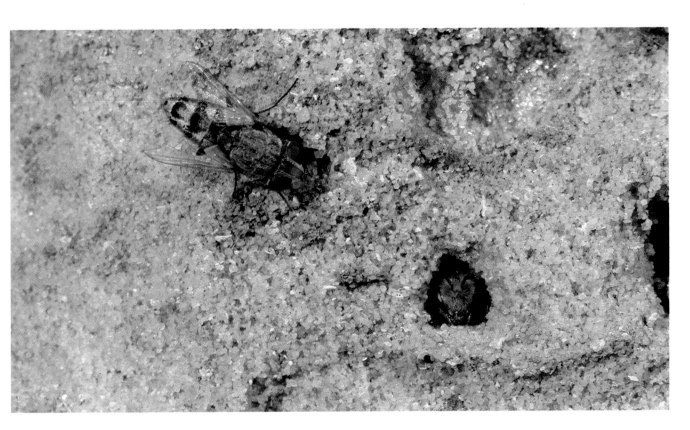

Later in the year, mining bees are attacked by another kind of fly called the satellite fly because the females closely follow female bees when they return to the nest. There the fly waits until the bee flies out again to collect pollen and nectar from flowers. Then

*A satellite fly waits for a bee to vacate her nest so that it can lay a larva on her food store.*

the satellite fly enters the nest and lays a single larva. This feeds on the food stored by the mother bee, and the bee larva dies of starvation.

## Wasp and Bee Mimics

Next time you see some flowers, take a look at the insects busily feeding there. Some of them may be wasps and bees. If you take a closer look many of the insects will turn out to be flower flies. Their bright black and yellow markings make them look like wasps or bees. But the number of wings gives the game away. Bees and wasps have two pairs of wings each; flower flies, being flies, have only one pair of wings.

The flower flies have a good reason to mimic wasps and bees. Female and worker wasps and bees each have a sting. Insect-eating birds and lizards learn to expect a painful sting if they peck at these brightly-colored insects. Bees and wasps use these colors as a warning and the flower flies have made use of this. They avoid being eaten because the birds are fooled into thinking they are stinging insects.

*This furry flower fly, drinking the nectar of hogweed flowers, looks and behaves just like a bumblebee.*

Some flower flies mimic bumblebees. Besides looking like bumblebees, they also sound like them. If

disturbed, they lie on their sides, waving one of their middle legs as a threat, just like a worker bumblebee.

*Two flower flies feeding on a teasel flower. Their striped abdomens make them look like wasps.*

# 6
# Some Unusual Flies

*A West Indian giant fly next to its pupal case. Notice the other tunnels made by the larvae.*

## West Indian Giants and Worm Lions

One of the world's largest flies lives on the islands of the West Indies and in South America. The larva of this giant fly spends its life boring away through solid wood, on which it feeds. It makes tunnels 12 mm (half an inch) wide and up to 18 cm (7 in) deep. The head bears a pair of very strong jaws. The back end is covered with an armored plate which is almost exactly the same size as the burrow and keeps enemies from getting at the rest of the soft-bodied larva. The armored plate also bears a pair of breathing holes and some gills. The larva can breathe through its gills if the tunnel becomes water-logged after heavy rain. The armored plate may also be used as a kind of shovel to get rid of all the chewed wood that the larva digs out when burrowing.

When the larva is fully grown, it pupates in the tunnel. The pupa is active and can crawl around. Just before the adult is due to emerge, the pupa sticks its head end out of the tunnel, and the adult can then come out into the open air.

Below *A West Indian giant fly larva in its tunnel. It has strong jaws to bite through wood.*

*A worm lion is the larva of a kind of snipe fly. It makes a pit in sandy soil to trap small insects to eat.*

Worm lions are very strange. They are the larvae of a kind of snipe fly. The adults prey on other insects. The larvae make traps by digging little pits in sandy soil and living at the bottom of them. They eat any insects that fall into this trap.

# 7
# The Enemies of Flies

*Crab spiders hide in flowers and pounce on insects they land to feed. This flower fly will be sucked dry.*

Flies are eaten by many animals and by plants too. Spiders are probably the best known enemies of flies. Every day millions of flies are caught in the sticky webs of spiders. Frogs and lizards catch and eat flies. Chameleons, which live in the warmer parts of the world, stalk insects in trees and bushes. Chameleons have long, sticky tongues, which can quickly dart out to pick up unwary insects.

Tree shrews catch almost any kind of insect, and they eat vast numbers of flies. A great many insect-eating birds eat flies. Flycatchers are birds that specialize in catching insects in flight. Vultures are not often thought of as insect eaters but the Egyptian vulture often eats large numbers of fly larvae, which feed on rotting animals in Africa.

Flies have two kinds of plant enemies: those that live inside them as parasites and those that actually trap them. The parasitic plants are all

**fungi**. One special kind attacks only flies. The fungus lives inside the body of the fly and slowly digests it.

Several different kinds of plants eat insects, including flies. The sundew grows in marshy places. It has special leaves covered with sticky tentacles that give out a sweet nectar. Flies land on the leaf to eat the nectar and are trapped in sticky glue. Slowly, the tentacles bend over and trap the fly. Then they produce juices to digest it.

The venus's-fly-trap uses special leaves, hinged in pairs, which produce nectar. When a fly lands on a leaf, it may touch a fine trigger hair. The two leaves snap shut, trapping the fly. It is then digested by the plant's juices.

*A fly infected with fungus.*

*A fly on a venus's-fly-trap.*

# Glossary

**Abdomen**   The rear of the three body parts of an insect, containing the stomach and the sex organs.

**Antennae**   The two feelers on the head of an insect. They contain the sense of smell, touch and, in some flies, a sense of hearing.

**Aphids**   Small insects, that suck the juices from plants.

**Fungi**   Simple types of plants without green coloration, such as mushrooms and molds.

**Hosts**   Animals that are the victims of parasites.

**Larva**   The form of an insect that emerges from the egg.

**Mating**   The joining of a male and a female animal so that the female's eggs are fertilized.

**Nectar**   A sweet liquid made by flowers.

**Ovipositor**   The egg-laying tube of a female insect.

**Parasitoid**   An insect that lives as a parasite of another insect, eventually killing it.

**Pollen**   The male sex cells of flowering plants, produced as a dusty powder by the male parts of a flower.

**Pollinator**   An animal, usually an insect, which accidentally fertilizes a plant by carrying pollen from the male parts of one flower to the female parts of another.

**Pupa**   The stage between larva and adult in insects, when the larva is broken down and reorganized to form the adult.

**Puparium**   The final skin of the larva of some kinds of flies; it forms a hard case around the pupa.

**Scavengers**   Animals that eat dead animals and garbage.

**Siphon**   A tube-like growth of the body through which many water-living insects breathe.

**Sperm**   The male sex cells.

**Spiracles**   In insects, breathing holes connected by a fine network of tubes that take oxygen to all parts of the body.

**Thorax**   The middle part of the three body parts of insects. The thorax bears the wings and the legs.

**True flies**   Members of a large group of insects that have only one pair of wings.

# Finding Out More

The following books will tell you more
about flies:

Boy Scouts of America. *Insect Life.* Irving,
TX: Boy Scouts of America, 1973.
Brandt, Keith. *Insects.* Mahwah, NJ:
Troll Associates, 1985.

Burton, Maurice. *The Life of Insects.*
Morristown, NJ: Silver Burdett, 1979.
Horton, Casey. *Insects.* New York: Franklin
Watts, 1984.
Fichter, George S. *Insect Pests.* New York:
Western Publishing, 1966.

# Index

## Picture Acknowledgments

All photographs from Oxford Scientific Films by the following photographers:

T. Allen 34; G.I. Bernard *frontispiece*, 9, 15 (bottom), 18, 19, 20, 23, 29, 31, 38, 39, 43 (left); J.A.L. Cooke 10, 15 (top), 16, 36, 40, 41 (left), 43 (right); M.P.L. Fogden 42; B. Frederick *cover*, 28; S. Morris 32; P. O'Toole 30, 37; P. Parks 14; A. Ramage 12, 17, 24, 25, 27 (bottom), 41 (right); D. Shale 21, 22; T. Shepherd 27 (top); D. Thompson 35; G. Thompson 33; N. Woods 8. All artwork by Wendy Meadway.